We should like to emphasize that the proposals made in this Report are specifically intended for the short-run period ahead, when higher education and the nation face urgent and immediate problems. The Carnegie Commission has sought to build upon the best features of existing programs and to recommend forms of aid which can be revised or replaced at any time, with the minimum of disruption to long-range planning, as better solutions are evolved through experience and research. Longer-run answers may ultimately be found in different kinds of support programs, and through innovations in educational structure, curriculum, and technology. But we cannot afford to defer the meeting of important national needs for academic quality and the extension of equality of opportunity while we continue our search for the long-run answers.

Carnegie Commission on Higher Education

Quality and equality: new levels of federal responsibility for higher education

A SPECIAL REPORT AND RECOMMENDATIONS BY THE COMMISSION

DECEMBER 1968

Andrew S. Thomas Memorial Library
MORRIS HARVEY COLLEGE, CHARLESTON, W. VA.

66414

McGRAW-HILL BOOK COMPANY
New York   St. Louis   San Francisco
London   Sydney   Toronto   Mexico   Panama

Table of contents

379.12
C215g

Foreword

1. **The nation's needs for higher education** 1
2. **Higher education's potential to meet the needs** 3
   Growth in size 3
   Growth in functions 5
   Rising costs 5
   Sources of funds 7
   Further federal support necessary to achieve goals of quality and equality 8
3. **The federal concern with higher education** 11
4. **Forms of federal support** 15
5. **Federal aid proposals** 17
   Student aid and related institutional grants 17
      Educational opportunity grants 18
      Recommendation 19
      Supplementary matching grants 20
      Recommendation 21
      Federal scholarship grants to institutions 21
      Recommendation 22
      Work-study program 22
      Recommendation 23
      Counseling and information program 23
      Recommendation 24
      Graduate talent search and development program 25
      Recommendation 25
      Doctoral fellowship program 26
      Recommendation 26
      National student loan bank 27
      Recommendation 29
      Part-time students 30
   Cost-of-education supplements to institutions 30
      Recommendation 30
   Medical education 32
      Recommendation 33
   Construction 36
      Recommendation 37
   Research 39
      Recommendation 40
   Special programs 41
      Recommendation 41
   National Foundation for the Development of Higher Education .. 43
      Recommendation 45

Conclusion 49

Foreword

In early 1967 the Carnegie Foundation for the Advancement of Teaching created a 15-member Commission on Higher Education to examine and make recommendations regarding the many vital issues facing higher education in the United States as we approach the year 2000. The Carnegie Foundation made clear to the Commission that it was not being asked to speak *for* higher education but rather *about* higher education and its needs and contributions in relation to the nation's social concerns and purposes.

The Commission then mapped out these major areas of higher education for study and investigation: structure, function, and governance; innovation and change; demand, resources, and expenditures; and efficiency in the use of resources. Research projects have already been initiated in several of these areas, and studies being conducted elsewhere are under review. The Commission will issue a final report containing its findings and recommendations at the conclusion of its activities several years from now.

Because of the urgency of some problems in the sphere of higher education and the need for early action, the Commission has decided to issue special reports on such topics as soon as data are available to indicate desirable short-run measures and the Commission has had the opportunity to clarify its views and to develop specific recommendations.

This Report, *Quality and Equality: New Levels of Federal Responsibility for Higher Education,* is the first in the series. The Commission hopes that it will prove useful and persuasive to those members of the 1969 Congress of the United States and of the executive branch who have key responsibilities in the area of higher education.

The recommendations in this Report are supported by all the present members of the Carnegie Commission on Higher Education. Although individual members differed occasionally on details and wording, there was surprising unanimity on the need for, and the general levels of, federal aid and on the broad directions of implementation.

It should be pointed out that Mr. Roy E. Larsen, Chairman of the Executive Committee of Time, Inc., and an original member of the Commission, found it necessary to resign in mid-1968 because of the pressure of other commitments. We wish to record here our deep appreciation of his valuable contributions to the early planning sessions of the Commission and to our initial considerations of the topic of federal aid to higher education.

We wish also to express our gratitude for the many helpful suggestions of those consulted during the development of our proposals.

Finally, we wish to thank the members of our staff, and particularly Miss Virginia Smith, for their assistance in the preparation of this Report.

RALPH M. BESSE
Chairman of the Board
The Cleveland Electric Illuminating Company

JOSEPH P. COSAND
President
The Junior College District of St. Louis

WILLIAM FRIDAY
President
University of North Carolina

DAVID D. HENRY
President
University of Illinois

THEODORE M. HESBURGH, C.S.C.
President
University of Notre Dame

CARL KAYSEN
Director
Institute for Advanced Study at Princeton

KATHARINE E. McBRIDE
President
Bryn Mawr College

JAMES A. PERKINS
President
Cornell University

CLIFTON W. PHALEN
Chairman of the Executive Committee
Marine Midland Banks

NATHAN M. PUSEY
President
Harvard University

DAVID RIESMAN
Professor of Social Sciences
Harvard University

THE HONORABLE
WILLIAM W. SCRANTON

NORTON SIMON
Hunt Food and Industries, Inc.

CLARK KERR
Chairman

1: The nation's needs for higher education

From the beginnings of the Republic, education at various levels has played a vital role in the building of a strong democratic society. At earlier stages in the nation's development, this role was chiefly the responsibility of the primary and secondary institutions. Now, as education through high school has become almost universal, as knowledge has increased, as the professional and intellectual demands of modern society have become ever more complex and exacting, the responsibility has shifted increasingly to America's colleges and universities.

Today, the nation looks to our institutions of higher learning to meet many of our most important needs:

More and more Americans, with aspirations for a better life, assume the necessity of a college education.

Equality of opportunity through education, including higher education, is beginning to appear as a realistic goal for the less privileged young members of our society.

The economy is dependent upon basic research and advancing technology, and upon the higher skills needed to make that technology effective, to assure national economic growth and well-being.

More managers, teachers, and professionals of all sorts are required to serve our complex society. More health personnel are essential to staff the fastest-growing segment of the national endeavor.

The cultural contributions of higher education take on wider dimensions as rising levels of education and growing affluence and leisure make possible greater concern with the quality of life in the United States.

Above all, the nation and the world depend crucially upon rigorous and creative ideas for the solution to profoundly complex issues.

What the American nation needs and expects from higher education in the critical years just ahead can be summed up in two phrases: quality of result and equality of access. Our colleges and universities must maintain and strengthen academic quality if our intellectual resources are to prove equal to the challenges of contemporary society. At the same time, the nation's campuses must act energetically and even aggressively to open new channels to equality of educational opportunity.

2: Higher education's potential to meet the needs

Does American higher education have the necessary resources to meet *at the same time* the nation's expectations for protection of academic quality and for expansion of equality of educational opportunity? Can our colleges and universities find ways to encourage and accommodate growing numbers of students, many of whom will need special financial and academic assistance, while preserving essential margins of academic excellence?

In January, 1968, the National Association of State Universities and Land-Grant Colleges had this to say about the response of public institutions to the shortage of resources:

> To maintain quality, they have raised student charges substantially, turned away qualified students, limited enrollment, and refused requests for urgently needed public service.

Three months later the Association of American Universities issued this statement:

> American higher education is experiencing critical and widespread financial pressures. Virtually every type of college and university faces a widening gap between annual income and the level of expenditures required to undertake needed expansion and improvement—or even, in many cases, to sustain normal operation.

To evaluate the present and potential financial strength of higher education, it is necessary to examine four essential factors: growth in size, growth in functions, rising costs, and sources of funds.

Growth in size

Higher education is currently encountering pressures created in large part by its own record of accomplishments. A century ago, enrollment in higher education in the United States was only about 50,000 students. Today's enrollment is almost 6 million students on a full-time equivalent (FTE) basis. More than half of this growth took place in the decade from 1958 to 1967. Estimates indicate that enrollment will pass 8 million by 1976, and this figure may well rise to 9 million if Carnegie Commission or other proposals are adopted to remove financial barriers for students from low-income families.

These enrollment data reflect not only the growing population of the United States and the growing share of that population in the younger age brackets, but also the rapidly increasing proportions of young people who seek higher education. A century ago, 2 percent of young Americans entered college. Now the figure is over 40 percent and is still rising.

Parental expectations or hopes of children's college attendance are now widespread. A Gallup poll shows that 97 percent of all parents questioned want their children to enter college. The national trend appears to be toward extending universal education beyond high school and through at least some years of higher education.

It should be noted, however, that the proportions of young people enrolled in higher education vary considerably from one part of the country to another. Percentages are more than twice as high for the Western states of Arizona, Utah, and California, as those for the Southern states of Mississippi, Georgia, South Carolina, and Alabama.

It is apparent that the nation's colleges and universities and those responsible for their financial support must provide new facilities for 3 million additional students by 1976–77. To fall short of this goal would be to limit the movement toward greater equality of access to higher education.

Enrollment will continue to rise after 1976–77 for about another decade, but at a slower rate, and will then level off until the year 2000. The heaviest costs of further expansion will be met in the period ending about 1980.

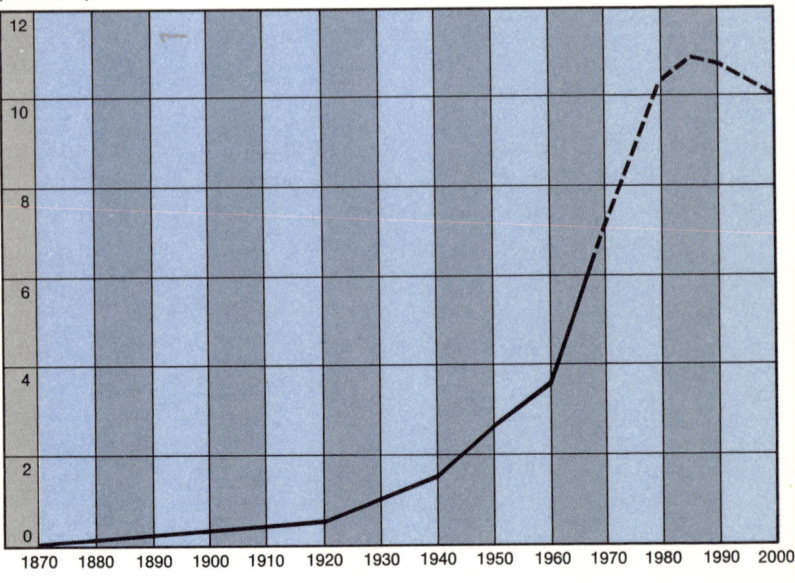

FIGURE 1

Enrollment in institutions of higher education

Growth in functions

Sheer numbers of students do not, of course, tell the entire story of institutional growth. Colleges and universities in the United States have also grown steadily in the number and complexity of functions they have assumed in response to both the expansion of knowledge and the needs of society.

Instruction has increased in total duration, in curricular range, and in specialization. Research has burgeoned. Graduate and professional programs have multiplied. Colleges and universities are performing a wide variety of important public services directed toward meeting civic and social problems.

This trend will continue in the future as higher education responds to new public needs. Today our institutions are being asked to extend their research efforts on the problems of the cities. They are expected to train additional doctors and medical support personnel to meet the nation's expanding activities in the important field of health care. There is a growing obligation to provide postdoctoral training and continuing education in a variety of fast-developing fields.

These expanding functions have brought our institutions of higher education to a central role in the well-being of our society. But they have also added greatly to the pressures of rising numbers of students and rising costs.

Rising costs

The continuing expansion of our higher education facilities will be expensive in any case. But the financial problems are made more severe by the fact that higher education costs per student are rising rapidly. Total institutional expenditures for higher education climbed from $5.2 billion in 1957–58 to about $17.2 billion in 1967–68, an increase of 231 percent as compared with a 119 percent increase in enrollments for the same period. It is estimated that expenditures of higher education institutions will total about $41 billion in 1976–77 for a projected FTE enrollment of 9 million students.

Institutional expenditures are the major costs but not the total costs of higher education. Certain government and private expenditures for higher education purposes are not reflected fully or at all in institutional spending data. Federal administrative costs for various higher education programs are not, of course, passed on to the institution. Federal student aid under the GI Bill and the

5

Social Security Act and some forms of state student aid go directly to the student, and only a portion of that aid enters the institutional revenue-expenditure data via tuition and institutional room-and-board payments. Expenditures of GIs and other students for books, supplies, differential living expenses, and other associated higher education costs which are incurred outside the institution also do not appear in the institutional data.

Unfortunately, the determination of the total cost of higher education is difficult and, inevitably, somewhat arbitrary, and no reliable estimates of the total cost are currently available. This Report, therefore, will rely primarily on use of the fairly well-established data on institutional expenditures for higher education. It is the institutional expenditure total that the Commission estimates will rise to $41 billion in 1976–77.

In terms of the gross national product (GNP), expenditures by higher education institutions rose from approximately 1 percent in 1957, when the GNP was $432 billion, to slightly more than 2 percent in 1967, when the GNP was $763 billion. Institutional expenditures will need to be about 3 percent by 1976–77, at which time the GNP will be about $1,400 billion.

Many factors aside from the general level of inflation have contributed to rising costs per student. Faculty salaries, which had lagged for some years, have been rising faster than the general level of wages and salaries. Graduate work has increased in importance, and it is more expensive. More sophisticated and costly research and teaching tools are required.

For many other activities of society, rising costs are offset in substantial part by accompanying rises in productivity. Unfortunately, higher education has not and perhaps cannot offset its rising costs in this manner. Despite improvements in college management and experiments in programmed learning and other new techniques, no major ways are likely to be found in the short run which will make it possible to educate more students at the same level of expenditures without lowering academic quality. The search for techniques to improve educational productivity without endangering quality should be actively pressed forward; as was indicated in the Foreword to this Report, efficiency in the use of resources is one of the major areas of higher education mapped out for study by the Carnegie Commission. In the meantime, it is inevitable that costs per student will continue to rise.

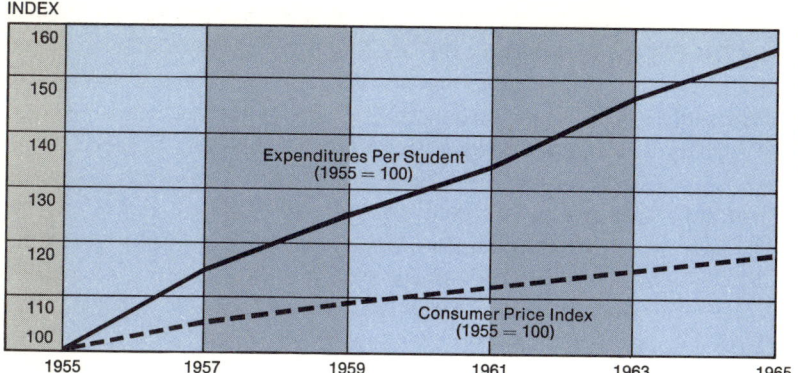

FIGURE 2

Comparative rise of direct educational expenditures per student and consumer price index

Sources of funds

Higher education has long received some federal assistance, but the chief financing burden has been borne by state and local governments and the private sector. It is a striking testimonial to their faith in higher education that they have financed the enormous expansion to date, and that they are girding to do still more in the future. But there are limits.

Many state and local governments whose expenditures for higher education are already large would experience great difficulties in providing the additional support needed, both because of tax base limits and because of the other essential needs for public funds. Some states whose past expenditures for higher education have lagged should, of course, provide additional funds in substantial amounts. State support, however, has been a falling share, and it is realistic to expect it to fall still more.

Private resources, initially the major support for all higher education in this country, have provided about half of the institutional funds required for higher education in recent years. With expectations of rising per capita income, and with a relatively high income elasticity for educational expenses, private resources should continue to provide half of the expanded financial support for higher education—a heavy increase in absolute dollar amounts. It would be unrealistic to assume, however, that the private share can be increased in percentage terms over the next few years. This continued heavy reliance on private sources of support for higher education will be helpful to the preservation of autonomy and diversity in American higher education.

The federal government, with revenue available from the graduated income tax, is the major source now realistically able to raise its general revenues faster than the gross national product and thus able to offset the decline in the share borne by the states.

State, local, and private sources combined now pay about four-fifths of total higher education institutional expenditures, and the federal government pays one-fifth. While the absolute amounts paid by all sectors must continue to rise substantially, federal support levels in dollar terms will need to triple in the immediate future. The federal government's proportionate share of institutional support will need to rise from about one-fifth at present (almost $4 billion) to about one-third (over $13 billion) of the new total by 1976–77.

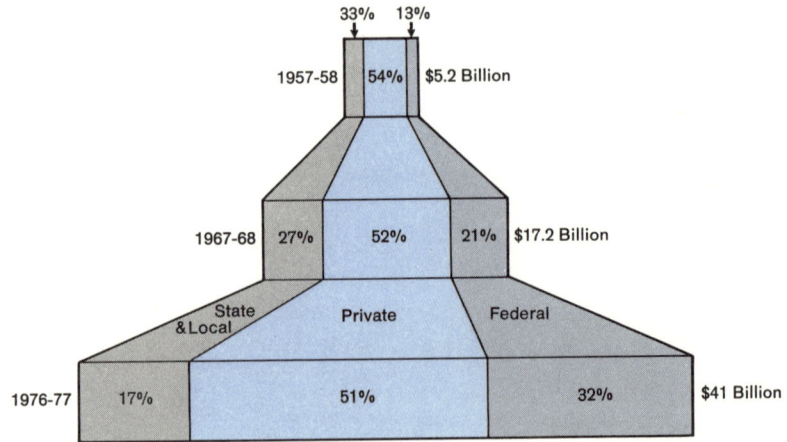

FIGURE 3

Sources of funds expended by institutions of higher education, 1957–58, 1967–68, and 1976–77 (based on federal aid proposals in this report)

	1957–58		1967–68		1976–77	
	$ BILLIONS	%	$ BILLIONS	%	$ BILLIONS	%
State and local ..	1.7	33	4.7	27	7	17
Private	2.8	54	9.0	52	21	51
Federal	0.7	13	3.5	21	13	32
Total	5.2	100	17.2	100	41	100

Further federal support necessary to achieve goals of quality and equality

The Carnegie Commission believes a much greater federal investment is now essential if the growth of higher education is not to be curbed at the very time that the national need is so crucial for our best ideas and intellectual skills and for the broadest possible extension of equality of opportunity.

The severity of the problem is not uniform throughout higher education. Some institutional levels, some geographical areas, some kinds of institutions face more critical financial needs than others. Overall data may disguise the serious nature of the problems for many institutions and students. Capacity not fully utilized in some areas is nevertheless inaccessible to students being turned away from overcrowded local facilities if those students lack the financial means to travel to and live in other areas. Available financial resources at one institution or system of institutions are not transferable to others. Improved resource planning on one campus does not help solve financial shortages at another whose resources are already being inventively utilized to the maximum.

Although the financial impacts have differed, most institutions have by now had to absorb so many of these pressures that formerly available margins in facilities and resources have been depleted. These institutions are now being forced to choose among the alternatives of limiting enrollments, raising tuition fees, postponing expansion and new programs, or allowing quality to deteriorate. These alternatives are already being employed in varying degrees throughout higher education.

The adverse effects upon national needs are all too clear. Enrollment limitations and higher tuition fees (unless offset by grants and loans to those with low incomes) penalize first the very group of students for whom the goal of greater equality of opportunity is intended. Postponing expansions and new programs means deferring activities that may be among the most urgently needed at the present, such as the training of additional health science personnel or research on urban problems. Sacrificing general quality weakens the vital intellectual resources of the nation.

We believe that national needs in the areas of academic quality and equality of opportunity require new levels of federal support for higher education.

3: The federal concern with higher education

The well-being of higher education in the United States is a concern which the federal government shares with state and local governments and private individuals and organizations charged with primary responsibility for our colleges and universities. Higher education fulfills purposes which are national as well as regional and local, and public as well as private, in their scope and impacts. College graduates and holders of advanced and professional degrees are highly mobile geographically; they are participants in what is essentially a continental market. And it is precisely this broad market which has been an important factor in the prosperity of the nation as a whole. Thus it is appropriate that federal as well as

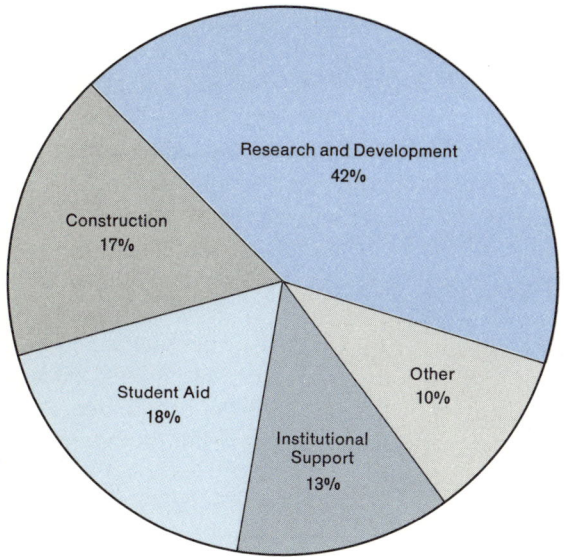

FIGURE 4

Estimated obligations for higher education and related activities, 1967–68

Federal funds of $698 million for research centers managed by universities, $412 million for veterans' education, $409 million for construction loans, and $266 million for student loans are not included.

	$ BILLIONS
Research and development	1.45
Construction	0.57
Student aid	0.62
Institutional support	0.44
Other	0.37
Total	3.45

state and local support be given to the nation's institutions of higher education.

The federal government has, in fact, helped to support higher education over the years, with such federal actions as the land-grant movement of post-Civil War days, National Youth Administration programs for needy students during the Depression of the 1930s, aid for science programs during and after World War II, student aid to returning veterans through the GI Bill, and in recent years a growing range of measures to assist various aspects of higher education.

By 1967–68, federal aid given directly to institutions of higher education and to various student aid programs (not including veterans' and social security education benefits) had reached a total of almost $4 billion and was being channeled through a variety of programs to some 2,100 colleges and universities and several hundred thousand students throughout the United States.

But the nation's needs for higher education, and thus the needs of higher education for more resources, continue to climb. In the next few years, federal support levels should be tripled if the federal government is to assist state and local governments and the private sector in expanding higher education as an essential investment in the nation's future.

In urging these support levels, the Carnegie Commission is not unmindful of the other and pressing national needs for which federal funds must be allocated. In the broad area of education alone, there are urgent calls for aid at primary and secondary levels and for vocational training. Institutions involved in these levels of education face an array of urgent problems, and we warmly support higher levels of aid, including more federal assistance, for these other segments of education. Our focus in this Special Report, however, is the financial problems of our colleges and universities. We believe that federal aid to higher education warrants a high priority among other federal programs, both because of the importance of the specific national needs which higher education serves and because intellectual resources are indispensable to the resolution of so many other high-priority national issues.

The proposed net increase in federal aid to institutions of higher education by 1976–77 is approximately $10 billion over current federal support levels. Projected growth of federal revenue would indicate that the net increment to federal revenue (over "work load" increases in costs) will reach about $70 billion by 1976–77. Thus the proposed increase in federal aid to institutions of higher education would require one-seventh of the expected additions to available federal revenues over the next few years for new programs. The Commission is convinced that the federal government can meet this new level of responsibility for higher education without penalty to other urgent national priorities.

4: Forms of federal support

The Carnegie Commission believes that federal support of higher education should be based upon the related concerns of contributions to the national welfare and to the vitality and effectiveness of the institutions of higher education themselves.

The forms of federal aid employed should satisfy the following requirements:

> Draw forth to the extent possible, rather than merely replace, state and private support
>
> Provide for flexibility and periodic reevaluation to determine whether changing national needs warrant reallocations
>
> Assist both public and private institutions—the latter, of course, for nonsectarian purposes only
>
> Improve equality of educational opportunity for all able young people
>
> Rely heavily upon market processes through free student choice of institution and field of study
>
> Preserve institutional autonomy and integrity
>
> Encourage diversity
>
> Provide an incentive for innovation
>
> Maintain among distinguished institutions of learning a margin for excellence, a premium for quality
>
> Use competitive principles in the support of academic quality, through nationwide competition for graduate fellowships and for institutional proposals in various special program fields

It is the Carnegie Commission's judgment that the best immediate means of federal aid to higher education are:

> Grants and loans to individual students to move toward the nation's goal of equal educational opportunity
>
> Support to institutions to meet increased costs of expanding enrollment and to strengthen areas of particular national concern
>
> Extension of support for research, for construction, and for special programs

Two other widely discussed approaches are considered by the Commission as far less desirable than extension of existing programs. One such approach, tax credits to parents of children in college, would not aid low-income families where the need is greatest. Another, general subsidies to the several states, would fail to provide the coordination and perspective necessary to assure expansion of programs of primary national concern.

5: Federal aid proposals

The following proposals are those which the Carnegie Commission believes will best meet the most urgent financing problems associated with higher education through 1976–77. While most of the recommendations would result in expansion or augmentation of existing programs, new programs suitable for use in a short-run period are also proposed. No attempt is made here to incorporate or comment upon all existing federal aid activities relating to higher education.

STUDENT AID AND RELATED INSTITUTIONAL GRANTS

The Carnegie Commission believes that one of the most urgent national priorities for higher education between now and 1976–77 is the removal of financial barriers for all youth who enroll in our diverse colleges and universities, whether in academic or occupational programs. A second important priority is support for talented graduate students who can meet the nation's needs for a wide variety of professionals, technical specialists, researchers, and college teachers.

The federal government presently provides limited amounts of student aid under a number of separate programs, some restricted to one or another major subject field, some based on need, some on ability, some channeled through the GI Bill. Today's graduating high school student often has difficulty in determining what student aid is available to him. Each program has separate requirements and applications. Often he must enroll in a college or university and then see if that institution still has funds available under particular programs. To replace these separate and limited programs (though not, of course, the GI Bill), the Commission proposes a substantially expanded program consisting of educational opportunity grants based on need, a work-study program, student loans, a counseling and information program, a graduate talent search and development program, and doctoral fellowships based on ability.

The Commission's program of student aid is based upon these premises:

1. Student aid must be adequate to remove effectively the financial barriers which now prevent many qualified students from entering or continuing higher education.

2. Basic grants supplemented by work-study payments should be scaled to differing educational expenses in the lower division, upper division, and graduate years. With the growth of the community

college movement and urban facilities, most students will be able to attend low-cost institutions near home for at least the first two years.

3. The grant program should be augmented by a loan program making possible greater flexibility in choice of college to the needy student and providing a readily available source of college financing with repayment deferred for all students regardless of need.

4. Maximum flexibility and fullest utilization of aid funds will be accomplished if the major portion of these funds is kept in one national reservoir and granted to individual students who exercise free choice of institution and disciplinary fields. If funds are allocated by institution or region or field, problems of over- and underuse will inevitably arise and require time-consuming and costly transfer procedures. The "national reservoir" approach has worked very successfully under the GI Bill. For administrative purposes, however, grant payments would be made to students by their selected institutions rather than directly by the government.

Educational opportunity grants

Equality of opportunity in the United States today is increasingly related to equality of access to education. And we have not yet achieved equality of access to education; financial barriers and racial barriers block the way for many potentially able young Americans. Almost half of the undergraduate college students in the United States now come from the country's highest family income quartile; only 7 percent come from the lowest income quartile.

Complete figures are not available for socioeconomic distribution of graduate enrollment, but fragmentary figures suggest that an even lower proportion of graduate students comes from the two lowest quartiles.

The proportion of Negroes in the American college population is less than half the proportion of Negroes in the population as a whole, and half the Negroes in college attend predominantly Negro colleges.

Financial barriers to higher education result in a demonstrable loss of national talent. In the highest socioeconomic quartile, 19 out of 20 students ranking in the top ability group (the highest 20 percent) enter college within five years after high school graduation; in the lowest socioeconomic quartile, only 10 out of 20 in the highest ability group enter college.

Although the federal government, in the past, has provided financial aid to college students through the GI Bill, loans, and student work programs in the Depression, it was not until the Higher Education Act of 1965 that a program of educational opportunity

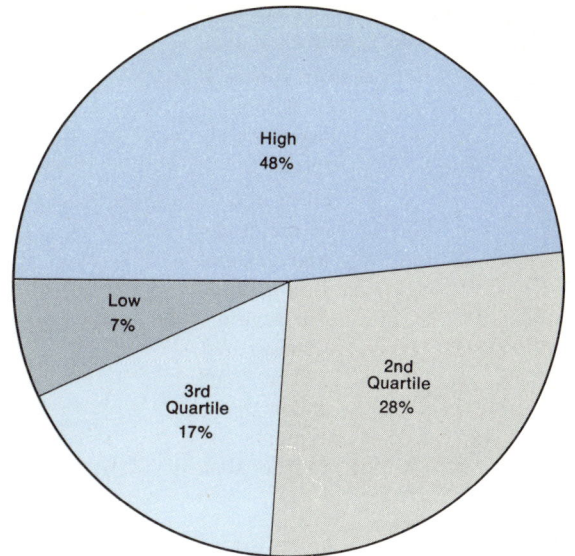

FIGURE 5

Percent undergraduate students enrolled full time by size of family income, 1966–67

APPROXIMATE FAMILY INCOME QUARTILE	AVERAGE FAMILY INCOME
High (above $10,000)	$16,016
Second ($6,000–$10,000)	8,359
Third ($3,000–$6,000)	5,549
Low (below $3,000)	2,321

grants was established. Under this program 225,000 undergraduate students from low-income families received grants in 1966–67. Adoption of a clear policy to remove financial barriers should make grants available to about 1.7 million students (27 percent of total enrollment) in 1970–71 and approximately 2.9 million students (32 percent of total enrollment) in 1976–77.

Recommendation:

The Commission recommends strengthening and expanding the present program of educational opportunity grants based on need by providing:

1. That the level of funding be increased so that all college students with demonstrated need will be assured of some financial aid to meet expenses at institutions which they select

2. That grants based on need be available for a period not to exceed four years of undergraduate study and two years of study toward a graduate degree

Determination of need. It will be necessary to derive a simple need formula based on such factors as total family income over the past several years, total family assets, and number and ages of children. The Commission assumes that a maximum grant would often be necessary at the lowest income quartile, that perhaps half of the maximum grant would be the average requirement at the second lowest quartile, and that only a few grants would be made to students from families on the lower borders of the upper half of the income range.

Amount of grants. Assuming full need, maximum grants would be:

   a. $750 per year to a student during his first two years of work toward an undergraduate degree or certificate

   b. $1,000 per year to a student during his third and fourth years of work toward an undergraduate degree

   c. $1,000 per year for a maximum of two years to a student working toward a graduate degree

No grant would be made unless the student is eligible for a grant in an amount of $200 or more.

It should be noted that the amounts in (*a*) and (*b*) above may be augmented by supplementary matching grants and work-study payments provided in the recommendations below.

Level of funding. It is estimated that the program of educational opportunity grants set forth above would require federal funding as follows:

YEAR	$ BILLIONS
1970–71	0.9
1971–72	1.0
1972–73	1.1
1973–74	1.3
1974–75	1.4
1975–76	1.6
1976–77	1.6

Supplementary matching grants

Institutions are expected to seek additional funds from private, state, and local government sources for undergraduate educational opportunity grants. It is estimated that over $600 million in student aid funds was obtained from these sources in 1966–67. It is not known what proportion of these student aid funds was used for grants to students from low-income families. To encourage commitment of more funds from these sources for such grants and to provide greater choice of selection of college for the student, the Commission proposes a program of supplementary matching grants.

Recommendation:

<u>The Commission recommends that an undergraduate student holding an educational opportunity grant and receiving added grants from nonfederal sources be given a supplementary federal grant in an amount matching the nonfederal grants but not exceeding one-half of the student's original educational opportunity grant.</u>

An upper-division student with full need might, for example, hold a $1,000 educational opportunity grant. If he were awarded an additional state or private grant of $400, he would thereby become eligible for a federal supplementary matching grant of $400, bringing his total grant level for the year to $1,800. If a holder of a $1,000 educational opportunity grant were to be given an added $700 from state or private sources, he could receive a federal supplementary matching grant of $500 (the upper limit of one-half of the amount of his original educational opportunity grant), for a total grant level of $2,200 per year.

Level of funding. It is estimated that this program would require federal funding as follows:

YEAR	$ MILLIONS
1970–71	110
1971–72	140
1972–73	180
1973–74	230
1974–75	280
1975–76	340
1976–77	380

Federal scholarship grants to institutions

The Commission recognizes that any formula for need applied on a nationwide basis may not adequately cover individual hardship cases. To provide some greater degree of flexibility in the allocation of grants to students with financial need, the Commission proposes that some additional scholarship funds be given directly to institutions where holders of educational opportunity grants are enrolled. The college or university would then allocate these funds to students as determined by the institution's own definition of student need.

Recommendation:

<u>The Commission recommends that each college and university be given a scholarship fund for needy students equal to 10 percent of the total sum of educational opportunity grants (not including supplementary matching grants) held by students at that institution.</u>

Level of funding. Federal funding requirements for this program are estimated as follows:

YEAR	$ MILLIONS
1970–71	90
1971–72	95
1972–73	105
1973–74	120
1974–75	135
1975–76	150
1976–77	160

Work-study program

During the Depression, the federally funded National Youth Administration provided payment for part-time jobs to more than 10 percent of all students then enrolled in higher education. More recently, the college work-study program was established. Originally under the Economic Opportunity Act of 1964, it was continued as a part of the Higher Education Act of 1965. The purpose of the program is to stimulate and promote part-time employment for students—particularly those from low-income families—who need the work to stay in school. Through federal grants to institutions of higher education, the program provides work opportunities on campus and in public or private nonprofit agencies engaged in community service off campus. Students may work an average of 15 hours a week while classes are in session and not more than 40 while they are not in session.

During fiscal 1968, 310,000 students participated in this program, the federal share costing an estimated $112.5 million. The work-study program has generated enthusiasm among participating students, colleges and agencies, especially at the state and community college levels. Significant numbers of economicaly disadvantaged youths are enabled to enter and stay in college. These students perform tasks important to academic institutions and agencies serving the community. In tangible and practical ways they develop an additional framework of relationships with the academic community. Work-study is one of the most valuable forms of student aid and ought to be incorporated in any federal program to assist students.

Recommendation:

<u>The Commission recommends that federal funds be provided to finance institutionally administered part-time employment for undergraduate students. Institutions should use these funds to enable students, who meet in general terms the federal need criteria, to earn up to $500 per year. Off-campus assignments of educational importance, such as tutorial work, should be encouraged.</u>

Because students from lower socioeconomic groups may experience educational disadvantages in their initial college years, it might be desirable to place some limits on their work-study program participation at the lower-division level. Upper-division students, and lower-division students to the extent consistent with their educational needs, should be encouraged to take part in the work-study program.

Level of funding. This program would require estimated levels of federal funding as follows:

YEAR	$ MILLIONS
1970–71	510
1971–72	540
1972–73	620
1973–74	700
1974–75	775
1975–76	850
1976–77	870

Counseling and information program

The National Defense Education Act of 1958 authorized establishment of a broad program throughout all levels of education for guidance, counseling, and testing of students and for identification and encouragement of able students to continue their education. One of the stated purposes of that program was to encourage students with outstanding aptitudes and ability to complete secondary school, take the necessary courses for admission to institutions of higher education, and enter such institutions. In 1959 $7.4 million was initially appropriated for the program. The appropriation for 1967 was $24.5 million.

The Commission believes, because of the importance of decisions made at the high school level about college attendance, that it is imperative to strengthen counseling and information programs. Students who possess the ability to go on to college-level academic work should be identified, assisted in finding the right college, and advised on the availability of financial aid. Identification of these students early in their high school careers would make it possible to channel them into curricula which would better equip them for higher education. Those with other interests and qualifications who can benefit either from further development before their prospects are clear or from more vocationally oriented education should be guided into courses at the appropriate institution. But not every high school graduate should be guided toward further formal education at that time, and this decision too is an important counseling responsibility.

The federal program should include support of research activities to develop better ways to identify qualified students, particularly those from disadvantaged groups. Federal training courses should be established for high school teachers and counselors to keep them up to date on financial aid, college programs, and career possibilities. Information centers should be established in metropolitan centers so that parents and students may obtain information about career possibilities and opportunities for higher education.

Colleges and universities should be encouraged to use a portion of their work-study program funds to enable their students to work with high school and elementary school students in various tutoring and counseling programs.

Recommendation:

The Commission recommends that the present federal aid program of guidance, counseling, and testing for identification and encouragement of able students be expanded to include the elements described above and that funding for the program be increased to $30 million in 1970–71, rising to $40 million in 1976–77.

Graduate talent search and development program

The nation's 2,300 institutions of higher education vary greatly, not only in function, but also in educational effectiveness. As a result, some students have earned their bachelor's degrees at institutions that have found it difficult, often because of financial pressures, to attain a desirable level of quality in their educational programs. Colleges of this type, often found in the economically depressed areas of the nation, may be the only facilities accessible to many students from low-income families and, in some sections of the country, to students from racial minorities. The developing institutions program, mentioned later in these proposals, is concerned with improving the quality of these colleges. But this improvement cannot be quickly achieved.

At the very time when the nation has growing needs for specialized personnel in health, welfare, technical, and professional fields and in elementary and secondary teaching, it is particularly unfortunate that some students who have completed their undergraduate training find that they are not adequately prepared to undertake graduate programs in these and other needed areas. It is equally unfortunate that some of these students come from the very groups of the population that need opportunities to participate more fully and at increasingly higher levels in the nation's work force.

As a partial remedy to this situation, the Commission urges that a federal program be funded under which certain universities, selected on the basis of specific program proposals, undertake the task of identifying potentially able graduates who have not received undergraduate training adequate to permit immediate pursuit of graduate studies. The programs could vary considerably in nature, but each would provide up to one year of intensive work to enable program participants to undertake their graduate studies more successfully. Students selected would receive a stipend based on need for the duration of the program.

Recommendation:

The Commission recommends that certain universities be selected on the basis of program proposals submitted to national panels to undertake specific graduate talent search and development programs, and that federal funding be made available for such programs in the amount of $25 million in 1970–71, rising to $100 million in 1976–77.

Doctoral fellowship program

For several years, various federal agencies have offered doctoral fellowships and traineeships to students selected largely on the basis of achievement. Grants of this type were made to over 30,000 doctoral students in 1967.

The Commission has recommended above that educational opportunity grants based on need should be made available to first-level graduate students for a maximum of two years during work toward a graduate degree. In addition, the Commission proposes a program of loans (see the recommendation below) to assist students at all levels of undergraduate and graduate study.

Because of the great importance of encouraging the most able of our young students to continue their graduate studies at the highest level, the Commission proposes a federally financed doctoral fellowship program based on ability for students in all fields of intellectual endeavor. This program would provide stipends to talented students working toward the Ph.D. or equivalent research doctorate degree during the intensive period of their research for the doctoral thesis.

Recommendation:

The Commission recommends establishment of a doctoral fellowship program with selection based upon demonstrated academic ability without reference to need, with fellowships in the amount of $3,000 annually for a maximum of two years to graduate students advanced to candidacy for a Ph.D. or equivalent research doctorate, the total number of such first-year fellowships to equal three-fourths of the national total of earned doctorates in the previous year.

Selection. Of the total number of fellowships to be awarded annually, half would be selected by national competition. The other half would be granted on the basis of allocations to institutions for certain departments or interdepartmental major programs designated by national panels of experts, and the institutions and departments would then apply their own ability criteria for selection of recipients. Selection would be extended into the social sciences and humanities and not limited to the sciences and health professions as is largely true at present.

Teaching assistantships. A graduate student holding a doctoral fellowship would be expected to devote full time to his academic work, but could be required by the university as a part of his degree program to hold a teaching assistantship and would be permitted to receive a teaching assistantship stipend from the university.

Level of funding. It is estimated that federal expenditures for this program would be:

YEAR	$ MILLIONS
1970–71	105
1971–72	110
1972–73	120
1973–74	130
1974–75	150
1975–76	160
1976–77	165

National student loan bank

The Commission's opportunity grant and work-study recommendations are designed to remove financial barriers to higher education for students from low-income families. However, this is not the only kind of student assistance that is needed in a situation of rising educational costs. Grant recipients might wish to attend institutions far from their homes or with high tuitions, at costs greater than the ceilings appropriate to a grant program based on need. For many middle-income families, especially those with several children in college, the burdens of meeting the costs of higher education out of current income are large. Older students increasingly assume the role of independent adults, and continued financial dependence on their families poses significant problems. For all these reasons, a widely available student loan program in which need is not a condition of eligibility is desirable as a supplement to the programs already proposed.

Economic considerations reinforce this judgment. On the whole, members of the population who have more education enjoy significantly higher earnings than those with less, and this correlation holds broadly over the whole educational spectrum. In one respect, therefore, higher education enhances the earning power of individuals, thus providing the economic basis for repayment of debts incurred to finance that education. In this sense such loans can be viewed as financing individuals' investments in productive though nontangible capital.

Further, the social benefits of higher education which affect the whole nation, over and above those accruing to the individuals receiving it, justify a federal government effort in this area. Additionally, higher incomes result in higher tax payments to the federal government.

The desirability of federal participation in loan programs has already been recognized in such past programs as the National Student Defense Loan program established in 1958 and the Guaranteed Loan program established in 1965. These together had outstanding loans of over a billion dollars by 1966–67.

However, the existing loan programs have important difficulties, the greatest of which is an inadequate level of funding. Others include limitations of eligibility in terms of need, 10-year repayment periods which have imposed high burdens and discouraged applicants, and ineffective attempts to make them recruiting devices for such occupations as teaching. What is needed is a much larger loan program of a quite different character.

A particular kind of loan program—namely, one with contingent repayment provisions under which the borrower contracts to pay back a fixed percentage of his income per $1,000 of debt each year for a long period (30 to 40 years)—has a number of important additional advantages which recommend it strongly over a conventional fixed-contract type of loan.

First, such a loan program would contribute significantly to a further equalization of educational opportunity. If the loan program as a whole were on a self-sustaining basis (as defined below), those whose posteducation incomes were highest would help pay for the costs of education of those whose posteducation incomes were lower. Since posteducation incomes are correlated among other things with incomes of the students' families, this would spread the cost of equalization of opportunity over both the current and the succeeding generations.

Second, the prospect of repayment would be a lesser deterrent under a contingent loan program than under a conventional fixed-contract program. This would lead to a wider use of loans since risks would be shared.

Third, the program would further emphasize the independence of the student by encouraging him to meet a larger proportion of his educational costs through a loan.

Certain difficulties which such a contingent loan proposal appears to raise are manageable. Two, in particular, have received wide attention: the possibility of adverse selection of applicants that would prejudice the solvency of the program and the so-called negative dowry of college-educated women who marry and leave the labor force. Detailed studies of the design of such a program (for example, that by Karl Shell and others) show that these difficulties can be met. Further careful study and drafting of such a program are, however, highly necessary.

The Commission recommends this loan program as a supplement to our other proposals, rather than as the basic or sole program for both student and institutional support.

Recommendation:

<u>The Commission recommends that a federal contingent loan program be created for which all students, regardless of need, would be eligible. With interest figured on the basis of federal borrowing costs, the program should be self-sustaining, except for administrative costs which would be met out of appropriations. Undergraduates would be eligible to borrow up to $2,500 per year, and graduate students up to $3,500 per year, for educational purposes. No student should be entitled to receive more in loans, all types of grants, and work-study payments in any year than the costs of education, including subsistence costs, as officially recognized by the institution in which he is enrolled.</u>

The program would be administered through the institutions of higher education, which will have the relevant information on grants and work-study payments to loan applicants.

Level of funding. A loan program of this sort must be viewed as clearly experimental; it is difficult to predict the extent to which it will be used. But if loans are to be made available to students without reference to need, it will be necessary to have the initial level of funding for the loan program high enough to eliminate any requirements for setting priorities among loan applicants. The Commission suggests that funding be made available to provide student loans totaling $2.5 billion in 1970–71, possibly increasing to as much as $5 billion in new student loans in 1976–77.

It is also difficult to predict the level of federal expenditures which would be required by this loan program. Although designed to be self-supporting, the program would require, particularly in the initial years, annual federal appropriations amounting to perhaps 5 percent of new loans committed that year for administrative costs and contingencies. This would amount to about $125 million in 1970–71, rising to $250 million in 1976–77.

Part-time students

Growing requirements for retraining during a person's lifetime and the probability that low-income students will have to work part-time suggest that the importance of part-time enrollment may increase in the future. All the programs recommended above are stated in terms of full-time students. The programs should, however, through the implementing legislation, be adapted to provide proportional aid to part-time students.

COST–OF–EDUCATION SUPPLEMENTS TO INSTITUTIONS

The proposed expansion of financial aid programs to make it possible for more students to attend universities and colleges will add to the present financial problems of these institutions. The full costs of education are not met through tuition payments. Moreover, the increase in numbers of disadvantaged students will tend to raise per-student instructional costs, because many of these students will need special educational assistance such as tutoring, counseling, and perhaps remedial training in special areas. Cost considerations should not be permitted to discourage colleges and universities from effectively recruiting and assisting potentially able young people no matter what their socioeconomic background might be.

At the doctoral level, the gap between tuition levels and full instructional costs is even greater. To some extent, this problem has been recognized in the past through federal programs which provide cost-of-education supplements to institutions attended by students holding federal graduate fellowships.

The Commission believes that this concept should be continued for the doctoral fellowship program and extended to the educational opportunity grant program as well.

Recommendation:

<u>The Commission recommends that the federal government grant cost-of-education supplements to colleges and universities based on the numbers and levels of students holding federal grants enrolled in the institutions.</u>

Amounts of grants. Accredited colleges and universities, and institutions deemed potentially eligible for accreditation except for their recent date of establishment, would receive the following amounts for each federal grant holder enrolled:

STUDENT LEVEL	1970–71	RISING TO	1976–77
Lower division	$ 525		$ 750
Upper division	700		1,000
First-level graduate	1,050		1,500
Doctoral	3,500		5,000

Educational assistance programs. As the student aid program brings into higher education a greater number of disadvantaged students, the problem of providing them with special educational assistance such as counseling and tutoring will become increasingly important. The Commission assumes that a portion of the cost-of-education supplement would be used by the institution to undertake programs giving special attention to the educational needs of students who, largely because of socioeconomic factors, have been under an educational disadvantage.

Cost-of-education supplements as guides to future institutional support programs. These supplements could be used by the institutions at their own discretion to meet general operating costs. Thus they would provide some useful body of experience with general federal support of institutions—experience which could be used as a basis for consideration of the many proposals now being made for such institutional grants. The cost-of-education supplement program is proposed to meet immediate short-run needs, but it will also give the Commission and others both time and valuable data for analysis of the impacts, benefits, and problems involved in proposed programs for long-range institutional support and in the particular formulas being suggested for such programs.

This experience will augment the valuable consideration and study which have already been given to broad programs of institutional support by state study groups such as that proposed for New York and by several education associations. Statements of the various education associations have been reprinted in the Carnegie Commission publication *Alternative Methods of Federal Funding for Higher Education,* prepared by Ronald Wolk. In addition, the American Council on Education has recently issued a comparison of several proposed formulas for institutional grants.

The Commission hopes and expects that many students with grants would be drawn into the smaller colleges across the nation, where they would receive more individual attention and have a better opportunity to participate in the life of the total campus community. Many of these colleges would have the capacity to receive more students if they were given financial support to offset, in part, their added costs. They would thus also have a greater opportunity to diversify their student bodies, as so many of them now wish to do.

Level of funding. It is estimated that federal expenditures for cost-of-education supplements would be:

YEAR	$ BILLIONS
1970–71	1.13
1971–72	1.28
1972–73	1.53
1973–74	1.94
1974–75	2.17
1975–76	2.51
1976–77	2.71

The Carnegie Commission hopes in the near future to make a study of and recommendations on state support to private colleges and universities.

MEDICAL EDUCATION

Medical and health services education is the one major subject area in higher education that the Carnegie Commission has singled out for specific federal aid proposals. The reasons are several: the great needs of the nation in the health field, the growing public concern with these needs as evidenced by Medicare and the many state and local health programs, the high cost of medical training facilities, the fact that new medical education facilities are needed to serve geographical regions without reference to state boundaries, and, finally, the high mobility of medical school graduates, many and even most of whom do not remain to practice within the states that provided their instruction.

It is estimated that facilities to provide spaces for about 75 percent more medical students will be required by 1976–77 to meet the nation's rapidly growing need for medical services over and above the spaces available in 1966, when Medicare came into operation. In contrast to the rapid increase of enrollments in most other fields of higher education, the supply of medical school graduates has grown relatively slowly since the 1920s, and it is apparent that vigorous new efforts must be made to provide more training facilities and to encourage more students to undertake training. At the present time, 20 percent of the new doctors starting practice in the United States each year have received their training abroad, and sometimes it is of a distinctly lower quality than that provided by medical schools in the United States. Additionally, health care is not now adequately available in many rural areas and urban ghettos.

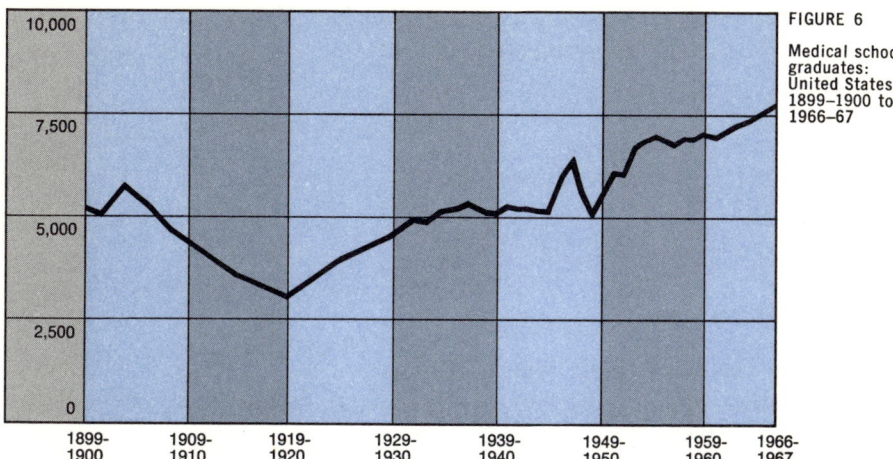

FIGURE 6

Medical school graduates: United States, 1899–1900 to 1966–67

Instructional and capital outlay costs for medical schools far outstrip the levels in other schools of professional education, including schools in which other health personnel are trained; and financing the major part of the needed expansion of such facilities from state and private resources is almost impossible.

Studies now underway give some promise that reorganization of medical education and of medical practice itself can lead to reduced costs of both medical education and medical care. Federal funds should be made available to support the development of expanded training programs for health support personnel. But these possibilities do not provide full solutions to the financing problems confronting medical education.

The federal government has been undertaking increasing levels of support for medical school construction ($18 million in 1966–67 and $55 million in 1967–68) and training ($42 million in 1966–67 and $53 million in 1967–68), but the Carnegie Commission believes higher federal levels are required.

Recommendation:

The Commission recommends establishment of a substantial program of federal aid for medical education and health services for the purposes of:

> Stimulating expansion of capacity at existing medical schools
>
> Planning additional medical schools distributed on a geographical basis to provide needed service to areas not now served
>
> Expanding educational facilities and developing new programs for the training of medical care support personnel
>
> Increasing availability of health services in the community of the medical school and the quality of health care delivery

Student aid. A student aid program for medical students should be adopted to provide grants on the basis of need in amounts up to $3,500 per year for four years, with free choice of institution.

It should be noted that medical students also have access to loans under the expanded loan program recommended above.

Institutional payments. Payments to institutions would be equal to the sum of the following amounts:

> 1. The institution's enrollment of students working toward the M.D. multiplied by $4,000
>
> 2. That portion of the enrollment working toward the M.D. in excess of such enrollment in the fall of 1966 multiplied by $2,000
>
> 3. The total number of residents and interns multiplied by $2,250, provided that no individual student shall be counted for more than four years, and provided further that the resident and intern program is conducted under the auspices of an accredited medical school either at its own or at an affiliated hospital

The amounts in (1) and (2) above should be adjusted for medical schools with three-year programs to enable those schools to receive the same amount of institutional aid as four-year schools.

Institutions would be free to use these institutional payments for support of any program which has as its major purpose the instruction of medical students.

Construction funds. Construction funds should be made available at the level of 100 percent for creation of new places, with additional funds for renovation and replacement.

Start-up grants. Start-up grants should be made available for non-construction costs for approximately 20 new medical schools at the rate of four per year for five years, not to exceed $10 million per school. These schools should be located in geographical areas not now adequately served by existing medical schools, with a sufficient population base to warrant a medical school, and with a university capable of providing a good environment for a medical school.

Community health service programs. Federal support should be made available for development of programs by medical schools designed to extend the availability and effectiveness of community health programs.

Training of support medical personnel. Federal funds should be made available for programs designed to increase the number of support medical personnel. Such personnel can be trained comparatively quickly and inexpensively. In some fields, such as pediatrics, they can assume a substantial share of the services now performed by M.D.s if they are given proper supervision by an M.D.

Level of funding. It is estimated that federal expenditures for the medical and health services education program outlined above would be:

YEAR	$ BILLIONS
1970–71	0.33
1971–72	0.35
1972–73	0.37
1973–74	0.39
1974–75	0.42
1975–76	0.40
1976–77	0.43

Medical education today is undergoing more constructive self-examination than it has since the Flexner report of 1910 and more than is going on in any other field of higher education. This is both impressive and commendable. The new medical schools recommended here can take advantage of the new ideas being born. Expansion of existing schools can provide opportunities for the new types of training for new types of doctors and support personnel now being envisioned. The medical profession as a whole is welcoming expansion of personnel and experimentation in training of personnel and delivery of health care as never before, to its great credit and the nation's great advantage; and the medical students of today encourage these progressive tendencies.

This openness to new concepts and new horizons of service should be fully encouraged as the federal government extends the basic support to medical education which it has given so successfully in the past to medical research. The second great transformation of medical education and research (the Flexner report having given rise to the first) is now underway, and the United States once again will greatly benefit. The new schools of medicine can be new in program as well as in physical identity; the expanded schools can be greater in their variety and relevance to modern needs as well as greater in size. Medical schools are on the threshold of becoming as important to the quality of urban life as the colleges of agriculture under the land-grant movement have been to rural life.

New money can now be matched by new ideas. Both are important—but the new ideas are the more important. The Carnegie Commission hopes subsequently to make suggestions on the future of medical education and its financing, and fully realizes that better use of health care facilities and personnel is as important as the enlargement of facilities and personnel.

CONSTRUCTION

During the late 1950s and the 1960s the great surge in college enrollment led to a growing deficiency in facilities. It was in recognition of this deficiency that the Higher Education Facilities Act was passed in 1963. But the increased federal aid came late and at too low a level to close the gap. By 1967 college and university instructional facilities would have had to be expanded by 20 percent to provide fully adequate space for the new levels of enrollment. This continuing deficiency resulted, in part, from the federal budgetary stringency which led to decreasing levels of support for college construction at a time when enrollment continued to rise.

Projected levels of enrollment suggest a further increase in this deficiency unless levels of federal support under the Higher Education Facilities Act can be increased. To keep pace with expanding enrollment, while holding the existing deficiency at its 20 percent level, about $2 billion of federal funds should be available annually for college and university construction.

At present, funds are channeled principally into new construction. We believe more attention should be directed to the use of construction grants for renovation, an approach which might provide some additional facilities more quickly and at lower costs.

During the last academic year 72 new colleges were established. Many more new campuses will be needed over the next few years, and campuses of particular types.

The advance of the junior college movement over the last decade

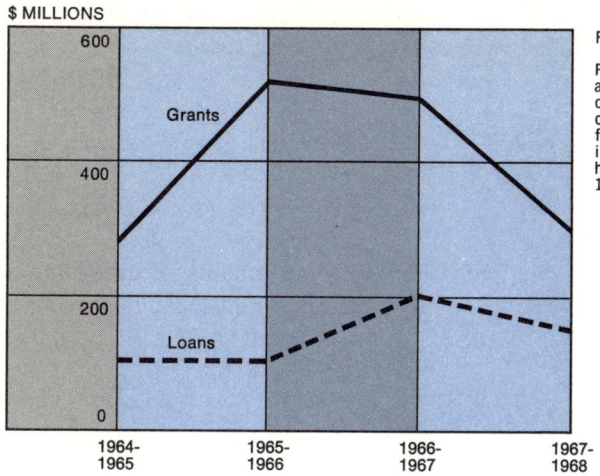

FIGURE 7

Federal grants and loans for construction of instructional facilities in institutions of higher education, 1964–1968

has greatly increased the accessibility of higher education to hundreds of thousands of American youth. A further extension of the growing junior college movement will continue this significant trend.

Colleges to serve the inner-city youth are urgently required in many of our major metropolitan areas. To meet this need, it is estimated that 500 community colleges and 50 urban four-year colleges should be established by 1976.

These new colleges, particularly in urban areas where land is expensive, will have heavier than usual initial costs. The Commission's proposals for construction aid include start-up grants for these institutions.

The Commission believes that support for construction is one of the most desirable mechanisms for channeling federal aid to colleges and universities. Such support carries with it very limited opportunities for control of educational policy; it increases the real assets of the nation; and, combined with matching requirements, it stimulates rather than replaces other sources of financial support for higher education.

Recommendation:

Construction grants:

1. The Commission recommends that the amount of federal grants for academic construction be increased from the present provision (two-fifths of construction costs for junior colleges and one-third for other institutions) to one-half of the total amounts required by

all institutions for construction, renovation, and replacement of facilities.

2. In addition, the Commission recommends that start-up grants be provided for planning and nonconstruction costs for new junior college and urban institutions, not to exceed $10 million per institution but averaging more nearly $1 million per institution.

Construction loans:

The Commission recommends that funding levels for the academic facilities construction loan program be increased to provide sufficient loan funds for an additional 25 percent of needed new construction costs.

It should be noted that institutions could thus finance up to 75 percent of new construction through a combination of federal grants and loans.

Level of funding. It is estimated that federal expenditures for construction grants and loan obligation levels would be:

YEAR	GRANTS ($ BILLIONS)	LOAN OBLIGATIONS ($ BILLIONS)
1970–71	1.26	0.53
1971–72	1.58	0.69
1972–73	1.86	0.83
1973–74	1.87	0.88
1974–75	1.88	0.89
1975–76	1.92	0.91
1976–77	1.22	0.61

Funding levels will continue to decline after 1976–1977 as enrollment levels stabilize in the 1980s.

The Commission recognizes that major improvements are possible in the intensity of space utilization and assumes that some of the estimated 20 percent deficiency across the nation can be offset by improved utilization.

Loans for student housing. For several years, federal loans for student housing have constituted an important form of federal aid to higher education. The Commission believes that this support is important to the educational effectiveness of many colleges and universities and urges continuation of the student housing loan program. This Report does not, however, include any recommendations on future levels of support for housing loans. The comparative emphasis on college housing and on privately supplied housing requires careful study campus by campus. College housing is of particular importance to the private liberal arts college with a residential character.

RESEARCH

One of the most essential functions of higher education is its contribution to the advance of knowledge in the nation. In recognition of this contribution the federal government has played a substantial role in providing major support for university-based research.

Since the federal government first undertook massive support of research in the universities during World War II, research expenditures have been a very large part of total federal expenditures on higher education. In the early postwar years, nearly half of the total federal support for higher education was directed to science research, and by 1958 the proportion had risen to two-thirds. Research now accounts for about one-third of the total federal funds flowing to higher education institutions.

More significantly, federal funding has been the primary source of support for university-based research activities. Today approximately three-quarters of all university research is federally financed. In some highly research-oriented universities, the figure is almost 90 percent.

The rate of increase of federal support to university research is thus the key element in its ability to expand. During the period from 1956 to 1962, federal support of academic research increased at a rate of about 25 percent per year, but the rate of increase has slowed sharply since 1962. Last year's increase in federal support for academic research was only 2 percent.

It is the Commission's belief that university research, and thus federal support for university research, must increase substantially over the next several years. Both the past increase (before the recent slowdown) and the proposed increase in federal support are based on several factors:

1. Enrollment of doctoral candidates has risen sharply over the last several years and will continue to rise at an average rate of 6.6 percent annually through 1975.

2. Costs of research, like costs of instruction, are rising more rapidly than the costs of the general economy.

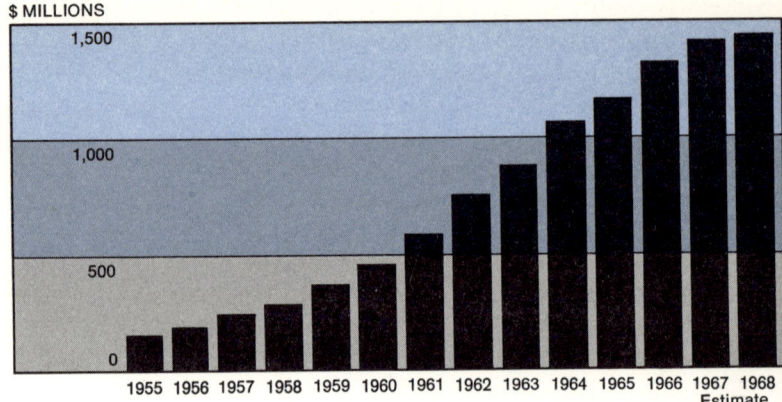

FIGURE 8

Federal obligations for research and development by universities and colleges, fiscal years 1955–1968

3. The new technology, which makes considerable expansion possible in the scope, nature, and quality of research, is also adding to the cost of research.

4. Critical social problems demand greater research efforts in many areas, including the social sciences.

Recommendation:

The Commission recommends that the level of federal funding for university and college research be increased over the next several years but with the annual rate of increase declining from 15 percent in 1970–71 to 10 percent in 1976–77. This rate of increase reflects expanding doctoral enrollments, use of more costly technology, and the need for expansion into new fields of research.

The Commission further recommends that a grant amounting to 10 percent of the total research grants received annually by an institution be made to that institution to be used at its discretion. The sum required for this purpose is to be included within the percentages noted immediately above.

Procedures. The present federal system for awarding research grants through multiple agencies based on review and determination of merit of each proposal seems to work relatively well; the Commission does not, therefore, recommend any basic change in the present procedure. However, it might be desirable for all granting agencies to adopt the practice now sometimes used of giving low priority to inclusion of funds for released faculty time, particularly at universities where the teaching load is relatively low;

conversely, efforts should be made to increase the teaching services of research personnel, and federal policy can encourage this.

The present system does sometimes make it difficult for colleges and universities to obtain federal research funds for small projects and for planning projects, and young faculty members may be under considerable disadvantage in competing for research funds. The proposed 10 percent supplementary grant to institutions would make it possible for them to provide grants for these purposes.

Level of funding. With one modification, the current level of federal funding for research can properly be used as a base for projecting desirable future levels of support. To some extent research funds are now used to provide traineeships for candidates for research doctorates. If the Commission's proposal for research doctoral fellowships is accepted, this need will be met directly through that program. In projecting future levels of federal funding for research, the Commission has started from a base lower than the present level of support, thus eliminating possible duplication between the present use of research funds and the proposed research doctoral fellowship program.

It is estimated that federal funds for support of research as outlined above would be:

YEAR	$ BILLIONS
1970–71	2.00
1971–72	2.30
1972–73	2.62
1973–74	2.96
1974–75	3.32
1975–76	3.68
1976–77	4.05

SPECIAL PROGRAMS

The federal government has been both sensitive and responsive to areas of particular need in higher education and has established a number of special programs to provide federal assistance for these areas.

Recommendation:

The Commission has not given consideration to all of these special programs, but does recommend increased funding for the following three programs: aid to developing institutions, library support, and international studies.

Aid to developing institutions

Many of the nation's existing colleges have failed to reach their full capability because of limitations of resources. If expanded educational opportunity is to be provided in the United States, these colleges must become full participants in the academic community. Since 1965, the Office of Education, through its developing-college program, has given some financial aid to such colleges, starting with $5 million in 1966 and increasing to $30 million in 1967. In too many instances the level of aid to institutions has not been sufficient to enable significant development, but only to tide them over for another year. Through this program some of these colleges might well be encouraged to combine with each other or with neighboring institutions. This program in its entirety can be of particular value to areas which are deficient in educational opportunity. The Commission recommends that funding for the developing college program be increased from its present level of $20 million to $100 million.

Library support

A basic tool of any college or university is its library. The current expansion of knowledge, with the resultant massive explosion in literature in all fields, has sharply increased the cost of even the minimal library for an undergraduate college. Major universities with their heavy emphasis on graduate education and research, face even greater increases in their annual library expenditures. The higher education law does provide support for college and research libraries, but the level of funding has been low. In 1966, although $50 million was authorized, only $10 million was appropriated. In 1967 and 1968 the appropriation was increased to $25 million. The Commission recommends that the full authorization of $50 million be made available in 1970–71 and be increased to $100 million by 1976, and that libraries which serve a regional need be given a high priority for grants under this program.

International studies

The years since World War II have witnessed an unprecedented growth in the number of new and independent nations in the world. The problems of their economic and political development and of their accommodation into the international sphere have accentuated the need for stronger university-based programs of international studies. The International Education Act of 1966 authorized some grant programs in this area, but no funds have yet been appropriated. More centers for comprehensive training and research both on specific geographical areas and on particular fields or issues in world affairs should be encouraged. The Commission recommends that the $90 million authorized for this program be appriated in 1970–71 and that funding be increased to $100 million by 1976–77.

Level of funding. The National Foundation for the Development of Higher Education would be initiating new special programs which, after their developmental phases, would be transferred to appropriate federal agencies.

Total funding for these special programs described above and for the others now in prospect might require $800 million by 1976–77.

NATIONAL FOUNDATION FOR THE DEVELOPMENT OF HIGHER EDUCATION

Research and graduate instruction in the nation's universities have been greatly strengthened over the past two decades, in large part because of substantial research support by the federal government. Parallel gains of this magnitude have not been made in other areas of higher education, such as undergraduate curriculum development, instructional techniques, utilization of resources, and new program areas.

The Commission believes that the federal government can play an extremely valuable role in encouraging developmental programs in higher education by providing initial funds for such undertakings. The continuing rise in the costs of higher education makes it particularly important to develop existing facilities to their greatest potential and to try out new methods and techniques in order to improve operational efficiency and quality. But many institutions find that they do not have a margin of funds for such undertakings.

The Commission proposes the establishment of a National Foundation for the Development of Higher Education to provide encouragement, advice, review, and financial support for institutional programs designed to provide new directions in curricula, strengthening of essential areas that have fallen behind or that have never been adequately developed because of inadequate funding, and development of programs to improve educational processes and techniques. The Foundation would be a governmental agency operating under the direction of a board and organized along the lines of the National Science Foundation.

It is intended that all programs funded through the Foundation would be short-run or developmental in character. Programs once experimented with, developed, and proved successful under the National Foundation would be transferred into the special programs category mentioned earlier and administered on a permanent basis by other agencies of the federal government, usually the Office of Education.

Examples of developmental programs which might be funded by the Foundation are the following:

Improvement of undergraduate education

Criticism of the quality of undergraduate education has become widespread during the past few years. The recent focus of national attention on research needs and associated graduate instruction has undoubtedly occasioned some neglect of the undergraduate area. In addition, many undergraduate students across the nation have evinced new interest in undergraduate programs which minimize the fragmenting effects of specialization and which emphasize relevance to the current problems of our society. A healthy mood of reform is evident on many campuses and could be encouraged through the National Foundation.

Services to elementary and secondary education

The quality of education at the primary and secondary levels has an obvious bearing on the number and quality of students who enter our colleges and universities, and it is particularly important in assuring greater equality of access to higher education. In recent years, institutions of higher education have begun to assume more responsibility for assistance to the earlier levels in the educational process, providing supplementary training programs for teachers, help in curriculum design, consultation in connection with school problems such as integration, and other similar services. The federal government has given support to these programs in particular areas. In 1967–68, for example, the National Science Foundation awarded grants of $46 million for teacher training programs in the sciences, and the Office of Education provided over $12 million for a program of experienced-teacher fellowships. The National Foundation could review new service programs, which through improving the quality of education at the primary and secondary levels would have valuable consequences for higher education as well.

Regional liberal arts centers

Many undergraduate liberal arts colleges have formed consortia to permit them to use more effectively the resources available to each institution. This development could be encouraged through the National Foundation. The Commission urges that federal funds be made available to regional liberal arts centers which would be established by groups of colleges for the purpose of increasing quality, scope, and diversity in undergraduate education, of stimulating more economical and effective use of administrative and teaching personnel, and of sharing library and computer facilities.

The new technology

The newly created program of Networks for Knowledge and ongoing programs providing financial assistance for computer use at universities and colleges should be continued. The National Foundation could be particularly helpful, however, in evaluating proposals for experimental or pilot programs designed to determine the effectiveness of new educational uses of the whole range of modern technology.

Urban-grant activities

The land-grant college movement had a significant effect on the nature of the public and, to some extent, the private university. Today, the pressing problems of the city are calling for a new evaluation of the university's relationship to the city.

If universities and colleges are to aid in the solutions of the complex problems of the inner city, they will have to develop new curricular programs and new concepts of public service. Such developmental programs, during their early phases, could be funded under the National Foundation.

Recommendation:

The Commission recommends establishment of a National Foundation for the Development of Higher Education whose functions would be to encourage, advise, review, and provide financial support for institutional programs designed to give new directions in curricula, to strengthen essential areas that have fallen behind or never been adequately developed because of inadequate funding, and to develop programs for improvement of educational processes and techniques.

Level of funding. The Commission suggests that the Foundation for the Development of Higher Education be funded at a level of approximately $100 million in 1970–71, rising to $200 million in 1976–77.

Conclusion

The Carnegie Commission has undertaken an independent analysis of the needs of higher education and the needs of the nation as related to the services of higher education. Our analysis has led to the conclusion that federal aid to higher education, beyond the needed expansion of existing programs, should be directed toward the meeting of two urgent national priorities.

One of these priorities is to achieve greater equality of opportunity for all able young people, both for their own benefit and for the benefit of the nation. Today, young persons whose families are in the top half of the income range have a three times greater chance of entering college than those whose families are in the lower half. We believe it is a realistic goal to improve this ratio to two to one by 1976, the two-hundredth anniversary of the Declaration of Independence, with its promise of equality. Our proposals would draw 1 million additional students into college attendance through what might be called a "Civilian Bill of Educational Rights" for qualified youth without adequate financial means.

The second priority is a substantial expansion of health service personnel. Specifically we recommend federal support to increase medical school places for the training of doctors by three-quarters by 1976 and to develop programs for training new types of medical support personnel. This will require the enlargement of existing medical centers and the creation of as many as 20 new centers.

We also propose the continuation and expansion of a number of existing programs: for construction—including start-up grants for 500 new two-year community colleges and 50 four-year urban colleges; for research—including substantial extension of support beyond the sciences; for the training of Ph.D.s in all academic areas rather than primarily in the sciences; and for new endeavors to strengthen the system of higher education—including the creation of a National Foundation for the Development of Higher Education, which will encourage experimental programs such as those for the improvement of undergraduate instruction and for urban-grant activities.

These new priorities and the expansion of existing programs will cost approximately $10 billion per year by 1976, or about one-seventh of the $70 billion in additional federal revenues prospectively available by that year for new national priorities. We recognize the many other valuable purposes for which this increment will be needed, but we consider that a one-seventh share for higher education is warranted.

Our proposals envision keeping the share of private funds for the support of institutions of higher education at their present level of one-half. We feel that this level of private support is important for the autonomy and diversity of higher education. To assure that federal support is given in forms compatible with this private emphasis, we recommend an expanded student aid program giving the student freedom of choice among institutions, a feature which proved so effective under the GI Bill of Rights. This freedom of choice would be further broadened through a proposed student loan bank.

The total governmental share would remain at one-half, with the federal portion rising and the state portion falling, as has been true for the past decade. The federal government has the greater ability to increase its contribution. Also the new emphasis on equality of opportunity, the increase in health care personnel, the training of Ph.D.s for employment throughout the nation, the support of scientific discovery, and the strengthening of the whole system of higher education as a great national resource all reflect increasing national concern and responsibilities.

The Commission's proposals anticipate that the percentage of the GNP spent through institutions of higher education will rise by one-half from 2 to 3 percent. In the past decade the percentage doubled, from 1 to 2 percent, as enrollments doubled, and it now seems reasonable that the percentage should rise by one-half in the period to 1976, when enrollments will rise by one-half. Throughout this period the forms of service to society are taking on new dimensions in response to changing needs of society. There have been and there will be more knowledge, more training, and more service as higher education provides the intellectual sources of technical and social advance.

The prospects beyond 1976 are not clear. But, as enrollments stabilize, it would seem likely that subsequent support will rise roughly with the rise in GNP and will not require a significantly higher percentage of the GNP. The period from 1956 to 1976 will be viewed as the great period of expansion for higher education—the period in which the tidal wave of students was accommodated, and adjustment was made to the impact of greatly augmented scientific research.

We believe that the nation has a great stake in a dynamic, healthy, and flexible system of higher education, and our recommendations are intended to add to the strength and the progress of the system as well as to make possible greater service to society. The major aims of the proposals are:

To provide student aid in sufficient amounts to assure that no qualified student must forgo or cut short his pursuit of higher education because of financial barriers

To assist institutions of higher education with funds for expansion of physical facilities and for added instructional costs to assure the necessary places for all qualified students

To encourage graduate training of professional personnel, with particular emphasis on medical education, to fill critical national needs for practitioners in the health sciences

To support the most talented Ph.D. candidates and the institutions that train them at levels which will preserve and enhance the highest academic quality

To continue support of university research, a function which has already contributed so greatly to the national welfare and which holds the best promise of solutions to new problems of vital public concern

To provide special aid for new directions in curricula, for important areas that have fallen behind through inadequate funding, and for programs to improve educational processes and techniques

The total cost of the various federal aid programs recomended in this Report would be almost $7 billion in 1970–71 and would rise to almost $13 billion in 1976–77. The current cost of comparable federal aid programs is about $3.5 billion. The federal share of the funding of higher education institutions would rise from 21 to 32 percent, and the state share would fall from 27 to 17 percent. The private share would remain at approximately 50 percent.

Even with the levels of federal support proposed here, state and private sources will find the financial burden of basic support of higher education extremely heavy over the decade ahead. Institutions of higher education for their part will find it absolutely essential to make the most efficient and economical use of their available resources, to exercise the utmost restraint and care in the provision of new programs and facilities, and to reexamine their budgetary standards and practices. The Commission believes that quality can be maintained during a difficult fiscal period by scrupulous evaluation of all current and proposed educational programs.

Federal policy toward higher education and support of higher education require constant and careful overall review. We recommend the establishment of a Council of Advisers on Higher Education attached to the White House to undertake studies and recommend policy on the model of the Council of Economic Advisers.

American higher education is today a basic national resource. It affects the hopes and aspirations of the total population.

ESTIMATED FEDERAL EXPENDITURES
FOR COMMISSION PROPOSALS, 1970–71 AND 1976–77
($ BILLIONS)

	1970–71	1976–77
STUDENT AID PROGRAMS	1.91	3.56
Educational opportunity grants	1.10	2.14
[Basic student grants]	[0.90]	[1.60]
[Supplementary matching grants]	[0.11]	[0.38]
[Institutional scholarship funds]	[0.09]	[0.16]
Work-study program	0.51	0.87
Counseling program	0.03	0.04
Graduate talent search	0.03	0.10
Doctoral fellowships	0.11	0.16
Loan program	0.13	0.25
COST-OF-EDUCATION SUPPLEMENTS	1.13	2.71
MEDICAL EDUCATION PROGRAM	0.33	0.43
Student aid	0.03	0.04
General support grants	0.23	0.35
Construction	0.07	0.04
CONSTRUCTION	1.26	1.22
RESEARCH	2.00	4.05
FOUNDATION FOR THE DEVELOPMENT OF HIGHER EDUCATION	0.10	0.20
SPECIAL PROGRAMS	0.30	0.80
TOTAL	7.03	12.97

ESTIMATED FEDERAL LOAN COMMITMENTS
UNDER COMMISSION PROPOSALS, 1970–71 AND 1976–77

	1970–71	1976–77
CONSTRUCTION	0.53	0.61
STUDENT LOANS	2.50	5.00

As education through high school has become almost universal, as knowledge has expanded, as the professional and intellectual demands of modern society have become ever more complex and demanding, the nation has looked increasingly to America's colleges and universities to meet many of our most important national needs:

For furtherance of individual aspirations
For equality of educational and thus economic and social opportunity
For scientific and technological advances to stimulate economic growth

For highly trained personnel to serve a complex society
For cultural enrichment of the quality of life
And for the ideas so crucial to solution of profoundly complex issues

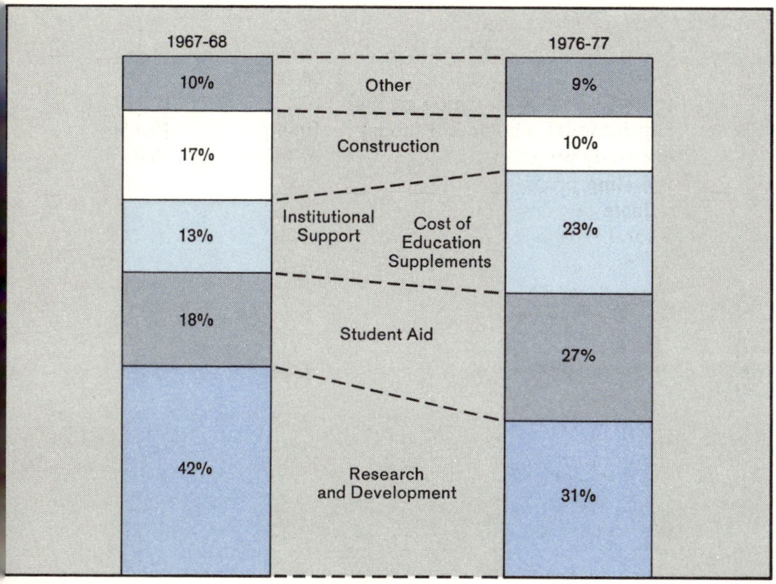

FIGURE 9

Percentage of federal aid to higher education by purpose, 1967–68 and 1976–77

	1967–68		1976–77
	10%	Other	9%
	17%	Construction	10%
	13%	Institutional Support / Cost of Education Supplements	23%
	18%	Student Aid	27%
	42%	Research and Development	31%

	1967–68 ($ BILLIONS)	1976–77 ($ BILLIONS)
Research and development	1.45	4.05
Student aid	0.62	3.60
Institutional support cost of education supplements	0.44	3.06
Construction	0.57	1.26
Other	0.37	1.25
Total	3.45	13.22

Note: The total of $13.22 billion for 1976–77 includes federal expenditures for Commission proposals and an estimated $250 million for certain programs of federal support to higher education institutions not covered in Commission proposals but expected to be continued. The 1967–68 institutional support figure includes an estimated amount for fellowship and traineeship program expenditures through institutions of higher education which are retained by institutions to defray partially the costs of the training programs.

What the American nation now needs from higher education can be summed up in two words: quality and equality. Our colleges and universities must preserve academic quality if our intellectual resources are to prove equal to the challenges of contemporary life. And the campuses must act boldly to open new channels to equality of educational opportunity.

But these essential national needs will not be fully met unless the federal government assumes new levels of responsibility for higher education. The Carnegie Commission believes that a much greater federal investment is now essential if the growth of higher education is not to be curbed at the very time that the national need demands our best ideas and intellectual skills and the broadest possible extension of equality of opportunity.

70 731 G C 53 1